The Ma

By Ki

JOHN, by the grace of God King of England, Lord of Ireland, Duke of
Normandy and Aquitaine, and Count of Anjou, to his archbishops, bishops, abbots, earls, barons, justices, foresters, sheriffs, stewards, servants, and to all his officials and loyal subjects, Greeting.

KNOW THAT BEFORE GOD, for the health of our soul and those of our
ancestors and heirs, to the honour of God, the exaltation of the holy Church, and the better ordering of our kingdom, at the advice of our reverend fathers Stephen, archbishop of Canterbury, primate of all England, and cardinal of the holy Roman Church, Henry archbishop of
Dublin, William bishop of London, Peter bishop of Winchester, Jocelin
bishop of Bath and Glastonbury, Hugh bishop of Lincoln, Walter Bishop
of Worcester, William bishop of Coventry, Benedict bishop of Rochester, Master Pandulf subdeacon and member of the papal household,
Brother Aymeric master of the knighthood of the Temple in England, William Marshal earl of Pembroke, William earl of Salisbury, William earl of Warren, William earl of Arundel, Alan de Galloway constable of
Scotland, Warin Fitz Gerald, Peter Fitz Herbert, Hubert de Burgh seneschal of Poitou, Hugh de Neville, Matthew Fitz Herbert, Thomas
Basset, Alan Basset, Philip Daubeny, Robert de Roppeley, John Marshal,
John Fitz Hugh, and other loyal subjects:

(1) FIRST, THAT WE HAVE GRANTED TO GOD, and by this present charter

have confirmed for us and our heirs in perpetuity, that the English Church shall be free, and shall have its rights undiminished, and its liberties unimpaired. That we wish this so to be observed, appears from the fact that of our own free will, before the outbreak of the present dispute between us and our barons, we granted and confirmed by
charter the freedom of the Church's elections - a right reckoned to be
of the greatest necessity and importance to it - and caused this to be
confirmed by Pope Innocent III. This freedom we shall observe ourselves,
and desire to be observed in good faith by our heirs in perpetuity.

TO ALL FREE MEN OF OUR KINGDOM we have also granted, for us and our
heirs for ever, all the liberties written out below, to have and to keep for them and their heirs, of us and our heirs:

(2) If any earl, baron, or other person that holds lands directly of the Crown, for military service, shall die, and at his death his heir shall be of full age and owe a `relief', the heir shall have his inheritance on payment of the ancient scale of `relief'. That is to say, the heir or heirs of an earl shall pay 100 for the entire earl's barony, the heir or heirs of a knight l00s. at most for the entire knight's `fee', and any man that owes less shall pay less, in accordance with the ancient usage of `fees'

(3) But if the heir of such a person is under age and a ward, when he
comes of age he shall have his inheritance without `relief' or fine.

(4) The guardian of the land of an heir who is under age shall take

from it only reasonable revenues, customary dues, and feudal
services.

He shall do this without destruction or damage to men or property. If
we have given the guardianship of the land to a sheriff, or to any
person answerable to us for the revenues, and he commits
destruction

or damage, we will exact compensation from him, and the land shall
be

entrusted to two worthy and prudent men of the same `fee', who
shall

be answerable to us for the revenues, or to the person to whom we
have

assigned them. If we have given or sold to anyone the guardianship
of

such land, and he causes destruction or damage, he shall lose the
guardianship of it, and it shall be handed over to two worthy and
prudent men of the same `fee', who shall be similarly answerable to
us.

(5) For so long as a guardian has guardianship of such land, he
shall

maintain the houses, parks, fish preserves, ponds, mills, and
everything else pertaining to it, from the revenues of the land
itself. When the heir comes of age, he shall restore the whole land
to

him, stocked with plough teams and such implements of husbandry
as the

season demands and the revenues from the land can reasonably
bear.

(6) Heirs may be given in marriage, but not to someone of lower
social

standing. Before a marriage takes place, it shall be' made known to
the heir's next-of-kin.

(7) At her husband's death, a widow may have her marriage portion and
inheritance at once and without trouble. She shall pay nothing for her
dower, marriage portion, or any inheritance that she and her husband
held jointly on the day of his death. She may remain in her husband's
house for forty days after his death, and within this period her dower
shall be assigned to her.

(8) No widow shall be compelled to marry, so long as she wishes to
remain without a husband. But she must give security that she will not
marry without royal consent, if she holds her lands of the Crown, or
without the consent of whatever other lord she may hold them of.

(9) Neither we nor our officials will seize any land or rent in
payment of a debt, so long as the debtor has movable goods sufficient
to discharge the debt. A debtor's sureties shall not be distrained
upon so long as the debtor himself can discharge his debt. If, for
lack of means, the debtor is unable to discharge his debt, his
sureties shall be answerable for it. If they so desire, they may have
the debtor's lands and rents until they have received satisfaction for
the debt that they paid for him, unless the debtor can show that he
has settled his obligations to them.

(10) If anyone who has borrowed a sum of money from Jews dies before
the debt has been repaid, his heir shall pay no interest on the debt
for so long as he remains under age, irrespective of whom he holds his

lands. If such a debt falls into the hands of the Crown, it will take nothing except the principal sum specified in the bond.

(11) If a man dies owing money to Jews, his wife may have her dower
and pay nothing towards the debt from it. If he leaves children that are under age, their needs may also be provided for on a scale appropriate to the size of his holding of lands. The debt is to be paid out of the residue, reserving the service due to his feudal lords. Debts owed to persons other than Jews are to be dealt with similarly.

(12) No `scutage' or `aid' may be levied in our kingdom without its general consent, unless it is for the ransom of our person, to make our eldest son a knight, and (once) to marry our eldest daughter. For
these purposes only a reasonable `aid' may be levied. `Aids' from the
city of London are to be treated similarly.

(13) The city of London shall enjoy all its ancient liberties and free customs, both by land and by water. We also will and grant that all other cities, boroughs, towns, and ports shall enjoy all their liberties and free customs.

(14) To obtain the general consent of the realm for the assessment of an `aid' - except in the three cases specified above - or a `scutage', we will cause the archbishops, bishops, abbots, earls, and
greater barons to be summoned individually by letter. To those who hold lands directly of us we will cause a general summons to be issued, through the sheriffs and other officials, to come together on a fixed day (of which at least forty days notice shall be given) and at a fixed place. In all letters of summons, the cause of the summons

will be stated. When a summons has been issued, the business appointed
for the day shall go forward in accordance with the resolution of those present, even if not all those who were summoned have appeared.

(15) In future we will allow no one to levy an `aid' from his free men, except to ransom his person, to make his eldest son a knight, and
(once) to marry his eldest daughter. For these purposes only a reasonable `aid' may be levied.

(16) No man shall be forced to perform more service for a knight's `fee', or other free holding of land, than is due from it.

(17) Ordinary lawsuits shall not follow the royal court around, but shall be held in a fixed place.

(18) Inquests of novel disseisin, mort d'ancestor, and darrein presentment shall be taken only in their proper county court. We ourselves, or in our absence abroad our chief justice, will send two justices to each county four times a year, and these justices, with four knights of the county elected by the county itself, shall hold the assizes in the county court, on the day and in the place where the
court meets.

(19) If any assizes cannot be taken on the day of the county court, as
many knights and freeholders shall afterwards remain behind, of those
who have attended the court, as will suffice for the administration of justice, having regard to the volume of business to be done.

(20) For a trivial offence, a free man shall be fined only in proportion to the degree of his offence, and for a serious offence correspondingly, but not so heavily as to deprive him of his livelihood. In the same way, a merchant shall be spared his merchandise, and a husbandman the implements of his husbandry, if they
fall upon the mercy of a royal court. None of these fines shall be imposed except by the assessment on oath of reputable men of the neighbourhood.

(21) Earls and barons shall be fined only by their equals, and in proportion to the gravity of their offence.

(22) A fine imposed upon the lay property of a clerk in holy orders shall be assessed upon the same principles, without reference to the
value of his ecclesiastical benefice.

(23) No town or person shall be forced to build bridges over rivers except those with an ancient obligation to do so.

(24) No sheriff, constable, coroners, or other royal officials are to hold lawsuits that should be held by the royal justices.

(25) Every county, hundred, wapentake, and tithing shall remain at its ancient rent, without increase, except the royal demesne manors.

(26) If at the death of a man who holds a lay `fee' of the Crown, a sheriff or royal official produces royal letters patent of summons for a debt due to the Crown, it shall be lawful for them to seize and list movable goods found in the lay `fee' of the dead man to the value of the debt, as assessed by worthy men. Nothing shall be removed until
the whole debt is paid, when the residue shall be given over to the

executors to carry out the dead man's will. If no debt is due to the Crown, all the movable goods shall be regarded as the property of the
dead man, except the reasonable shares of his wife and children.

(27) If a free man dies intestate, his movable goods are to be distributed by his next-of-kin and friends, under the supervision of the Church. The rights of his debtors are to be preserved.

(28) No constable or other royal official shall take corn or other movable goods from any man without immediate payment, unless the
seller voluntarily offers postponement of this.

(29) No constable may compel a knight to pay money for castle-guard if
the knight is willing to undertake the guard in person, or with reasonable excuse to supply some other fit man to do it. A knight taken or sent on military service shall be excused from castle-guard for the period of this service.

(30) No sheriff, royal official, or other person shall take horses or carts for transport from any free man, without his consent.

(31) Neither we nor any royal official will take wood for our castle, or for any other purpose, without the consent of the owner.

(32) We will not keep the lands of people convicted of felony in our hand for longer than a year and a day, after which they shall be returned to the lords of the 'fees' concerned.
(33) All fish-weirs shall be removed from the Thames, the Medway, and
throughout the whole of England, except on the sea coast.

(34) The writ called precipe shall not in future be issued to anyone in respect of any holding of land, if a free man could thereby be deprived of the right of trial in his own lord's court.

(35) There shall be standard measures of wine, ale, and corn (the London quarter), throughout the kingdom. There shall also be a standard width of dyed cloth, russett, and haberject, namely two ells within the selvedges. Weights are to be standardised similarly.

(36) In future nothing shall be paid or accepted for the issue of a writ of inquisition of life or limbs. It shall be given gratis, and not refused.

(37) If a man holds land of the Crown by `fee-farm', `socage', or `burgage', and also holds land of someone else for knight's service, we will not have guardianship of his heir, nor of the land that belongs to the other person's `fee', by virtue of the `fee-farm', `socage', or `burgage', unless the `fee-farm' owes knight's service. We will not have the guardianship of a man's heir, or of land that he holds of someone else, by reason of any small property that he may hold of the Crown for a service of knives, arrows, or the like.

(38) In future no official shall place a man on trial upon his own unsupported statement, without producing credible witnesses to the truth of it.

(39) No free man shall be seized or imprisoned, or stripped of his rights or possessions, or outlawed or exiled, or deprived of his standing in any other way, nor will we proceed with force against him,
or send others to do so, except by the lawful judgement of his equals
or by the law of the land.

(40) To no one will we sell, to no one deny or delay right or justice.

(41) All merchants may enter or leave England unharmed and without
fear, and may stay or travel within it, by land or water, for purposes
of trade, free from all illegal exactions, in accordance with ancient
and lawful customs. This, however, does not apply in time of war to
merchants from a country that is at war with us. Any such merchants
found in our country at the outbreak of war shall be detained without
injury to their persons or property, until we or our chief justice
have discovered how our own merchants are being treated in the country
at war with us. If our own merchants are safe they shall be safe too.

(42) In future it shall be lawful for any man to leave and return to
our kingdom unharmed and without fear, by land or water, preserving
his allegiance to us, except in time of war, for some short period,
for the common benefit of the realm. People that have been imprisoned
or outlawed in accordance with the law of the land, people from a
country that is at war with us, and merchants - who shall be dealt
with as stated above - are excepted from this provision.
(43) If a man holds lands of any `escheat' such as the `honour' of
Wallingford, Nottingham, Boulogne, Lancaster, or of other `escheats'
in our hand that are baronies, at his death his heir shall give us
only the `relief' and service that he would have made to the baron,
had the barony been in the baron's hand. We will hold the `escheat' in
the same manner as the baron held it.

(44) People who live outside the forest need not in future appear

before the royal justices of the forest in answer to general summonses, unless they are actually involved in proceedings or are sureties for someone who has been seized for a forest offence.

(45) We will appoint as justices, constables, sheriffs, or other officials, only men that know the law of the realm and are minded to keep it well.

(46) All barons who have founded abbeys, and have charters of English
kings or ancient tenure as evidence of this, may have guardianship of
them when there is no abbot, as is their due.

(47) All forests that have been created in our reign shall at once be disafforested. River-banks that have been enclosed in our reign shall
be treated similarly.

(48) All evil customs relating to forests and warrens, foresters, warreners, sheriffs and their servants, or river-banks and their wardens, are at once to be investigated in every county by twelve sworn knights of the county, and within forty days of their enquiry the evil customs are to be abolished completely and irrevocably. But we, or our chief justice if we are not in England, are first to be informed.

(49) We will at once return all hostages and charters delivered up to us by Englishmen as security for peace or for loyal service.
***here were some strange characters, not completely removed
(50) We will remove completely from their offices the kinsmen of Gerard de Ath, Peter, Guy, and Andrew de Chanceaux, Guy de Cigogne, and in
future they shall hold no offices in England. The

people in question are Engelard de Cigogn, Geoffrey de Martigny and his
brothers, Philip Marc and his brothers, with Geoffrey his nephew, and all their followers.

* As soon as peace is restored, we will remove from the kingdom all the foreign knights, bowmen, their attendants, and the mercenaries that have come to it, to its harm, with horses and arms.

* To any man whom we have deprived or dispossessed of lands, castles, liberties, or rights, without the lawful judgement of his equals, we will at once restore these. In cases of dispute the matter shall be resolved by the judgement of the twenty-five barons referred to below in the clause for securing the peace. In cases, however, where a man was deprived or dispossessed of something without the lawful judgement of his equals by our father King Henry or our brother King Richard, and it remains in our hands or is held by others under our warranty, we shall have respite for the period commonly allowed to Crusaders, unless a lawsuit had been begun, or an enquiry had been made at our order, before we took the Cross as a Crusader. On our return from the Crusade, or if we abandon it, we will at once render justice in full.

* We shall have similar respite in rendering justice in connexion with forests that are to be disafforested, or to remain forests, when these were first aforested by our father Henry or our brother Richard; with the guardianship of lands in another persons fee, when we have hitherto had this by virtue of a fee held of us for knights service by a third party; and with abbeys founded in another persons fee, in which the lord of the fee claims to own a right. On our return from the Crusade, or if we abandon it, we will at once do full justice to complaints about these matters.

* No one shall be arrested or imprisoned on the appeal of a woman for the death of any person except her husband.

* All fines that have been given to us unjustly and against the law of the land, and all fines that we have exacted unjustly, shall be

entirely remitted or the matter decided by a majority judgement of the twenty-five barons referred to below in the clause for securing the peace together with Stephen, archbishop of Canterbury, if he can be present, and such others as he wishes to bring with him. If the archbishop cannot be present, proceedings shall continue without him, provided that if any of the twenty-five barons has been involved in a similar suit himself, his judgement shall be set aside, and someone else chosen and sworn in his place, as a substitute for the single occasion, by the rest of the twenty-five.

* If we have deprived or dispossessed any Welshmen of lands, liberties, or anything else in England or in Wales, without the lawful judgement of their equals, these are at once to be returned to them. A dispute on this point shall be determined in the Marches by the judgement of equals. English law shall apply to holdings of land in England, Welsh law to those in Wales, and the law of the Marches to those in the Marches. The Welsh shall treat us and ours in the same way.

* In cases where a Welshman was deprived or dispossessed of anything, without the lawful judgement of his equals, by our father King Henry or our brother King Richard, and it remains in our hands or is held by others under our warranty, we shall have respite for the period commonly allowed to Crusaders, unless a lawsuit had been begun, or an enquiry had been made at our order, before we took the Cross as a Crusader. But on our return from the Crusade, or if we abandon it, we will at once do full justice according to the laws of Wales and the said regions.

* We will at once return the son of Llywelyn, all Welsh hostages, and the charters delivered to us as security for the peace.

* With regard to the return of the sisters and hostages of Alexander, king of Scotland, his liberties and his rights, we will treat him in the same way as our other barons of England, unless it appears from the charters that we hold from his father William, formerly king of Scotland, that he should be treated otherwise.

This matter shall be resolved by the judgement of his equals in our court.

* All these customs and liberties that we have granted shall be observed in our kingdom in so far as concerns our own relations with our subjects. Let all men of our kingdom, whether clergy or laymen, observe them similarly in their relations with their own men.

***Strange characters may have ended here.

SINCE WE HAVE GRANTED ALL THESE THINGS for God, for the better
ordering of our kingdom, and to allay the discord that has arisen between us and our barons, and since we desire that they shall be enjoyed in their entirety, with lasting strength, for ever, we give and grant to the barons the following security:

* The barons shall elect twenty-five of their number to keep, and cause to be observed with all their might, the peace and liberties granted and confirmed to them by this charter.

* If we, our chief justice, our officials, or any of our servants offend in any respect against any man, or transgress any of the articles of the peace or of this security, and the offence is made known to four of the said twenty-five barons, they shall come to us - or in our absence from the kingdom to the chief justice - to declare it and claim immediate redress. If we, or in our absence abroad the chief justice, make no redress within forty days, reckoning from the day on which the offence was declared to us or to him, the four barons shall refer the matter to the rest of the twenty-five barons, who may distrain upon and assail us in every way possible, with the support of the whole community of the land, by seizing our castles, lands, possessions, or anything else saving only our own person and those of the queen and our children, until they have secured such redress as they have determined upon. Having secured the redress, they may then resume
their normal obedience to us.

* Any man who so desires may take an oath to obey the commands of
the twenty-five barons for the achievement of these ends, and to join with them in assailing us to the utmost of his power. We give public and free permission to take this oath to any man who so desires, and at no time will we prohibit any man from taking it. Indeed, we will compel any of our subjects who are unwilling to take it to swear it at our command.
* If-one of the twenty-five barons dies or leaves the country, or is prevented in any other way from discharging his duties, the rest of them shall choose another baron in his place, at their discretion, who shall be duly sworn in as they were.
* In the event of disagreement among the twenty-five barons on any matter referred to them for decision, the verdict of the majority present shall have the same validity as a unanimous verdict of the whole twenty-five, whether these were all present or some of those summoned were unwilling or unable to appear.
* The twenty-five barons shall swear to obey all the above articles faithfully, and shall cause them to be obeyed by others to the best of their power.
* We will not seek to procure from anyone, either by our own efforts or those of a third party, anything by which any part of these concessions or liberties might be revoked or diminished. Should such a thing be procured, it shall be null and void and we will at no time make use of it, either ourselves or through a third party.

We have remitted and pardoned fully to all men any ill-will, hurt, or grudges that have arisen between us and our subjects, whether clergy
or laymen, since the beginning of the dispute.
We have in addition remitted fully, and for our own part have also pardoned, to all clergy and laymen any offences committed as a result
of the said dispute between Easter 1215 AD and the restoration of

peace.

In addition we have caused letters patent to be made for the barons,
bearing witness to this security and to the concessions set out above,
over the seals of Stephen archbishop of Canterbury, Henry archbishop
of Dublin, the other bishops named above, and Master Pandulf.

IT IS ACCORDINGLY OUR WISH AND COMMAND that the English Church shall
be free, and that men in our kingdom shall have and keep all these
liberties, rights, and concessions, well and peaceably in their
fulness and entirety for them and their heirs, of us and our heirs, in
all things and all places for ever.

Both we and the barons have sworn that all this shall be observed in
good faith and without deceit. Witness the above mentioned people and
many others.

Given by our hand in the meadow that is called Runnymede, between
Windsor and Staines, on the fifteenth day of June in the seventeenth
year of our reign .

***

[There were many missing spaces in this one, not sure I got them all]

Magna Carta 1215

John, by the grace of God, king of England, lord of Ireland, duke of

Normandy and Aquitaine, and count of Anjou, to the archbishops, bishops, abbots, earls, barons, justiciars, foresters, sheriffs, stewards, servants, and to all his bailiffs and liege subjects, greeting. Know that, having regard to God and for the salvation of our

soul, and those of all our ancestors and heirs, and unto the honor of God and the advancement of holy church, and for the reform of our realm, by advice of our venerable fathers, Stephen archbishop of

Canterbury, primate of all England and cardinal of the holy Roman Church, Henry archbishop of Dublin, William of London, Peter of Winchester, Jocelyn of Bath and Glastonbury, Hugh of Lincoln, Walter of

Worcester, William of Coventry, Benedict of Rochester, bishops; of master Pandulf, subdeacon and member of the household of our lord the

Pope, of brother Aymeric (master of the Knights of the Temple in England), and of the illustrious men William Marshall earl of Pembroke,

William earl of Salisbury, William earl of Warenne, William earl of Arundel, Alan of Galloway (constable of Scotland), Waren Fitz Gerald, Peter Fits Herbert, Hubert de Burgh (seneschal of Poitou), Hugh

de Neville, Matthew Fitz Herbert, Thomas Basset, Alan Basset, Philip

d'Aubigny, Robert of Roppesley, John Marshall, John Fitz Hugh, and

others, our liegemen.

1. In the first place we have granted to God, and by this our present charter confirmed for us and our heirs for ever that the English church

shall be free, and shall have her rights entire, and her liberties inviolate; and we will that it be thus observed; which is apparent from

this that the freedom of elections, which is reckoned most important and very essential to the English church, we, of our pure and unconstrained will, did grant, and did by our charter confirm and did obtain the ratification of the same from our lord, Pope Innocent III., before the quarrel arose between us and our barons: and this we

will observe, and our will is that it be observed in good faith by our heirs for ever. We have also granted to all freemen of our kingdom, for

us and our heirs for ever, all the underwritten liberties, to be had and held by them and their heirs, of us and our heirs for ever.

2. If any of our earls or barons, or others holding of us in chief by military service shall have died, and at the time of his death his heir shall be of full age and owe "relief" he shall have his inheritance on payment of the ancient relief, namely the heir or heirs of an earl, 100 pounds for a whole earl's barony; the heir or heirs of a baron, 100 pounds for a whole barony; the heir or heirs of a knight, 100 shillings at most for a whole knight's fee; and whoever owes less let him give less, according to the ancient custom officers.

3. If, however, the heir of any of the aforesaid has been under age and in wardship, let him have his inheritance without relief and without fine when he comes of age.

4. The guardian of the land of an heir who is thus under age, shall take from the land of the heir nothing but reasonably produce, reasonable customs, and reasonable services, and that without destruction or waste of men or goods; and if we have committed the wardship of the lands of any such minor to the sheriff, or to any other

who is responsible to us for its issues, and he has made destruction
or
waste of what he holds in wardship, we will take of him amends, and
the
land shall be committed to two lawful and discreet men of that fee,
who
shall be responsible for the issues to us or to him to whom we
shall assign them; and if we have given or sold the wardship of any
such land to anyone and he has there in made destruction or waste,
he
shall lose that wardship, and it shall be transferred to two lawful and
discreet men of that fief, who shall be responsible to us in like
manner as aforesaid.

5. The guardian, moreover, so long as he has the wardship of the
land,
shall keep up the houses, parks, fishponds, stanks, mills, and other
things pertaining to the land, out of the issues of the same land; and
he shall restore to the heir, when he has come to full age, all his
land, stocked with ploughs and "waynage," according as the season
of
husbandry shall require, and the issues of the land can reasonably
bear.

6. Heirs shall be married without disparagement, yet so that before
the
marriage takes place the nearest in blood to that heir shall have
notice.

7. A widow, after the death of her husband, shall forthwith and
without difficulty have her marriage portion and inheritance; nor shall
she give anything for her dower, or for her marriage portion, or for
the inheritance which her husband and she held on the day of the
death

of that husband; and she may remain in the house of her husband for
fourty days after his death, within which time her dower shall be assigned to her.

8. No widow shall be compelled to marry, so long as she prefers to live without a husband; provided always that she gives security not to
marry without our consent, if she holds of us, or without the consent of the lord of whom she holds, if she holds of another.

9. Neither we nor our bailiffs shall seize any land or rent for any debt, so long as the chattels of the debtor are sufficient to repay the debt; nor shall the sureties of the debtor be distrained so long as the principal debtor is able to satisfy the debt; and if the principal debtor shall fail to pay the debt, having nothing wherewith to pay it, then the sureties shall answer for the debt; and let them have the lands and rents of the debtor, if they desire them, until they are indemnified for the debt which they have paid for him, unless the principal debtor can show proof that he is discharged thereof as against the said sureties.

10. If one who has borrowed from the Jews any sum, great or small, die
before that loan can be repaid, the debt shall not bear interest while the heir is under age, of whomsoever he may hold; and if the debt fall
into our hands, we will not take anything except the principal sum contained in the bond.

11. And if any one die indebted to the Jews, his wife shall have her dower and pay nothing of that debt; and if any children of the deceased
are left underage, necessaries shall be provided for them in keeping

with the holding of the deceased; and out of the residue the debt shall
be paid, reserving, however, service due to feudal lords; in like manner let it be done touching debts due to others than Jews.

12. No scutage nor aid shall be imposed on our kingdom, unless by common counsel of our kingdom, except for ransoming our person, for
making our eldest son a knight, and for once marrying our eldest daughter; and for these there shall not be levied more than a reasonable aid. In like manner it shall be done concerning aids from the city of London.

13. And the city of London shall have all its ancient liberties and free customs, as well by land as by water; furthermore, we decree and
grant that all other cities, boroughs, towns, and ports shall have all their liberties and free customs.

14. And for obtaining the common counsel of the kingdom anent the assessing of an aid (except in the three cases aforesaid) or of a scutage, we will cause to be summoned the archbishops, bishops, abbots,
earls, and greater barons, severally by our letters; and we will moreover cause to be summoned generally, through our sheriffs and
bailiffs, all others who hold of us in chief, for a fixed date, namely, after the expiry of at least forty days, and at a fixed place; and in all letters of such summons we will specify the reason of the summons.
And when the summons has thus been made, the business shall proceed on
the day appointed, according to the counsel of such as are present, although not all who were summoned have come.

15. We will not for the future grant to any one license to take an aid from his own free tenants, except to ransom his body, to make his eldest son a knight, and once to marry his eldest daughter; and on each of these occasions there shall be levied only a reasonable aid.

16. No one shall be distrained for performance of greater service for a knight's fee, or for any other free tenement, than is due therefrom.

17. Common pleas shall not follow our court, but shall be held in some
fixed place.

18. Inquests of novel disseisin, of mort d'ancester, and of darrein presentment, shall not be held elsewhere than in their own county courts and that in manner following,--We, or, if we should be out of the realm, our chief justiciar, will send two justiciars through every county four times a year, who shall, along with four knights of the county chosen by the county, hold the said assize in the county court, on the day and in the place of meeting of that court.

19. And if any of the said assizes cannot be taken on the day of the county court, let there remain of the knights and freeholders, who were
present at the county court on that day, as many as may be required for
the efficient making of judgments, according as the business be more or
less.

20. A freeman shall not be amerced for a slight offense, except in accordance with the degree of the offense; and for a grave offense he
shall be amerced in accordance with the gravity of the offense, yet

saving always his "contentment;" and a merchant in the same way, saving
his "merchandise;" and a villein shall be amerced in the same way, saving his "wainage"--if they have fallen into our mercy: and none of the aforesaid amercements shall be impsed except by the oath of honest
men of the neighborhood.

21. Earls and barons shall not be amerced except through their peers,
and only in accordance with the degree of the offense.

22. A clerk shall not be amerced in respect of his lay holding except after the manner of the others aforesaid; further, he shall not be amerced in accordance with the extent of his ecclesiastical benefice.

23. No village or individual shall be compelled to make bridges at river-banks, except those who from of old were legally bound to do so.

24. No sheriff, constable, coroners, or others of our bailiffs, shall hold pleas of our Crown.

25. All counties, hundreds, wapentakes, and trithings (except our demesne manors) shall remain at old rents, and without any additional
payment.***here may be an error

26. If any one holding of us a lay fief shall die, and our sheriff or bailiff shall exhibit our letters patent of summons for a debt which the deceased owed to us, it shall be lawful for our sheriff or bailiff to attach and catalogue chattels of the deceased, found upon the lay
fief, to the value of that debt, at the sight of law-worthy men,

provided always that nothing whatever be then be removed until the debt
which is evident shall be fully paid to us; and the residue shall be
left to the executors to fulfil the will of the deceased; and if there
be nothing due from him to us, all the chattels shall go to
the deceased, saving to his wife and children their reasonable
shares.

27. If any freeman shall die intestate, his chattels shall be
distributed by the hands of his nearest kinsfolk and friends, under
supervision of the church, saving to every one the debts which the
deceased owed to him.

28. No constable or other bailiff of ours shall take corn or other
provisions from any one without immediately tendering money
therefor,
unless he can have postponement thereof by permission of the
seller.

29. No constable shall compel any knight to give money in lieu
of castle-guard, when he is willing to perform it in his own person, or
(if he cannot do it from any reasonable cause) then by another
responsible man. Further, if we have led or sent him upon military
service, he shall be relieved from guard in proportion to the time
during which he has been on service because of us.

30. No sheriff or bailiff of ours, or other person, shall take the
horses or carts of any freeman for transport duty, against the will of
the said freeman.

31. Neither we nor our bailiffs shall take, for our castles or for any
other work of ours, wood which is not ours, against the will of the
owner of that wood.

32. We will not retain beyond one year and one day, the lands of those
who have been convicted of felony, and the lands shall thereafter be
handed over to the lords of the fiefs.

33. All kiddles for the future shall be removed altogether from Thames
and Medway, and throughout all England, except upon the seashore.

34. The writ which is called praecipe shall not for the future
be issued to any one, regarding any tenement whereby a freeman may lose
his court.

35. Let there be one measure of wine throughout our whole realm; and
one measure of ale; and one measure of corn, to wit, "the London
quarter;" and one width of cloth (whether dyed, or russet, or
"halberget"), to wit, two ells within the selvages; of weights also let
it be as of measures.

36. Nothing in future shall be given or taken for a writ of inquisition
of life or limbs, but freely it shall be granted, and never denied.

37. If any one holds of us by fee-farm, by socage, or by burgage,
and holds also land of another lord by knight's service, we will
not (by reason of that fee-farm, socage, or burgage) have the wardship
of the heir, or of such land of his as is of the fief of that other;
nor shall we have wardship of that fee-farm, socage, or burgage,
unless such fee-farm owes knight's service. We will not by reason of
any small serjeanty which any one may hold of us by the service of
rendering to us knives, arrows, or the like, have wardship of his heir

of the land which he holds of another lord by knight's service.

38. No bailiff for the future shall, upon his own unsupported
complaint, put any one to his "law," without credible witnesses
brought
for this purpose.

39. No freeman shall be taken or imprisoned or disseised or exiled
or
in anyway destroyed, nor will we go upon him nor send upon him,
except
by the lawful judgment of his peers or by the law of the land.

40. To no one will we sell, to no one will we refuse or delay, right
or justice.

41. All merchants shall have safe and secure exit from England, and
entry to England, with the right to tarry there and to move about as
well by land as by water, for buying and selling by the ancient and
right customs, quit from all evil tolls, except (in time of war) such
merchants as are of the land at war with us. And if such are found in
our land at the beginning of the war, they shall be detained, without
injury to their bodies or goods, until information be received by us,
or by our chief justiciar, how the merchants of our land found in the
land at war with us are treated; and if our men are safe there, the
others shall be safe in our land.

42. It shall be lawful in future for any one (excepting always
those imprisoned or outlawed in accordance with the law of the
kingdom,
and natives of any country at war with us, and merchants, who shall
be
treated as is above provided) to leave our kingdom and to return,
safe

and secure by land and water, except for a short period in time of war,
on grounds of public policy--reserving always the allegiance due to us.

43. If any one holding of some escheat (such as the honor of Wallingford, Nottingham, Boulogne, Lancaster, or of other escheats which are in our hands and are baronies) shall die, his heir shall give
no other relief, and perform no other service to us than he would have
done to the baron, if that barony had been in the baron's hand; and we
shall hold it in the same manner in which the baron held it.

44. Men who dwell without the forest need not henceforth come before
our justiciars of the forest upon a general summons, except those who
are impleaded, or who have become sureties for any person or persons
attached for forest offenses.

45. We will appoint as justices, constables, sheriffs, or bailiffs only such as know the law of the realm and mean to observe it well.

46. All barons who have founded abbeys, concerning which they hold
charters from the kings of England, or of which they have long-continued possession, shall have the wardship of them, when vacant, as they ought to have.

47. All forests that have been made such in our time shall forthwith be disafforested; and a similar course shall be followed with regard

to river-banks that have been placed "in defense" by us in our time.

48. All evil customs connected with forests and warrens, foresters and warreners, sheriffs and their officers, river-banks and their wardens, shall immediately be inquired into in each county by twelve
sworn knights of the same county chosen by the honest men of the same
county, and shall, within forty days of the said inquest, be utterly abolished, so as never to be restored, provided always that we previously have intimation thereof, or our justiciar, if we should not be in England.

49. We will immediately restore all hostages and charters delivered to
us by Englishmen, as sureties of the peace or of faithful service.

50. We will entirely remove from their bailiwicks, the relations of Gerard Athee (so that in future they shall have no bailiwick in England); namely, Engelard of Cigogne, Peter, Guy, and Andrew of Chanceaux, Guy of Cigogne, Geofrrey of Martigny with his brothers, Philip Mark with his brothers and his nephew Geoffrey, and the whole
brood of the same.

51. As soon as peace is restored, we will banish from the kingdom all foreign-born knights, cross-bowmen, serjeants, and mercenary soldiers, who have come with horses and arms to the kingdom's hurt.

52. If any one has been dispossessed or removed by us, without the legal judgment of his peers, from his lands, castles, franchises, or from his right, we will immediately restore them to him; and if a dispute arise over this, then let it be decided by the five-and-twenty

barons of whom mention is made below in the clause for securing the

peace. Moreover, for all those possessions, from which any one has, without the lawful judgment of his peers, be endisseised or removed, by

our father, King Henry, or by our brother, King Richard, and which we

retain in our hand (or which are possessed by others, to whom we are

bound to warrant them) we shall have respite until the usual term of crusaders; excepting those things about which a plea has been raised,

or an inquest made by our order, before our taking of the cross; but as

soon as we turn from our expedition (or if perchance we desist from

the expedition) we will immediately grant full justice therein.

53. We shall have, moreover, the same respite and in the same manner
in rendering justice concerning the disafforestation or retention of those forests which Henry our father and Richard our brother afforested, and concerning wardship of lands which are of the fief of another (namely, such wardships as we have hitherto had by reason of a
fief which any one held of us by knight's service), and concerning abbeys founded on other fiefs than our own, in which the lord of the fief claims to have right; and when we have returned, or if we desist from our expedition, we will immediately grant full justice to all who complain of such things.

54. No one shall be arrested or imprisoned upon the appeal of a woman,
for the death of any other than her husband.

55. All fines made with us unjustly and against the law of the land,
and all amercements imposed unjustly and against the law of the
land,
shall be entirely remitted, or else it shall be done concerning them
according to the decision of the five-and-twenty barons of whom
mention
is made below in the clause for securing the peace, or according to
the
judgment of the majority of the same, along with the aforesaid
Stephen,
archbishop of Canterbury, if he can be present, and such others as
he
may wish to bring with him for this purpose, and if he cannot be
present the business shall nevertheless proceed without him,
provided
always that if any one or more of the aforesaid five-and-twenty
barons are in a similar suit, they shall be removed as far as
concerns
this particular judgment, others being substituted in their places
after having been selected by the rest of the same five-and-twenty
for
this purpose only, and after having been sworn.

56. If we have disseised or removed Welshmen from lands or
liberties,
or other things, without the legal judgment of their peers in England
or in Wales, they shall be immediately restored to them; and if a
dispute arise over this, then let it be decided in the marches by the
judgment of their peers; for tenements in England according to the
law
of England, for tenements in Wales according to the law of Wales,
and
for tenements in the marches according to the law of the marches.

Welshmen shall do the same to us and ours.

57. Further, for all those possessions from which any Welshman has,
without the lawful judgment of his peers, been disseised or removed by
King Henry our father or King Richard our brother, and which we retain
in our hand (or which are possessed by others, to whom we are bound to
warrant them) we shall have respite until the usual term of crusaders;
excepting those things about which a plea has been raised or an inquest
made by our order before we took the cross; but as soon as we return
(or if perchance we desist from our expedition), we will immediately
grant full justice in accordance with the laws of the Welsh and in
relation to the foresaid regions.

58. We will immediately give up the son of Llywelyn and all the
hostages of Wales, and the charters delivered to us as security for the
peace.

59. We will do toward Alexander, King of Scots, concerning the return
of his sisters and his hostages, and concerning his franchises, and his
right, in the same manner as we shall do toward our other barons of
England, unless it ought to be otherwise according to the charters
which we hold from William his father, formerly King of Scots; and this
shall be according to the judgment of his peers in our court.

60. Moreover, all these aforesaid customs and liberties, the
observance of which we have granted in our kingdom as far as
pertains
to us toward our men, shall be observed by all of our kingdom, as
well
clergy as laymen, as far as pertains to them toward their men.

61. Since, moreover, for God and the amendment of our kingdom
and for
the better allaying of the quarrel that has arisen between us and our
barons, we have granted all these concessions, desirous that they
should enjoy them in complete and firm endurance for ever, we give
and
grant to them the underwritten security, namely, that the barons
choose
five-and-twenty barons of the kingdom, whomsoever they will, who
shall
be bound with all their might, to observe and hold, and cause to be
observed, the peace and liberties we have granted and confirmed to
them
by this our present Charter, so that if we, or our justiciar, or our
bailiffs or any one of our officers, shall in anything be at fault
toward any one, or shall have broken any one of the articles of
the peace or of this security, and the offense be notified to four
barons of the foresaid five-and-twenty, the said four barons shall
repair to us (or our justiciar, if we are out of the realm) and, laying
the transgression before us, petition to have that transgression
redressed without delay. And if we shall not have corrected the
transgression (or, in the event of our being out of the realm, if our
justiciar shall not have corrected it) within forty days, reckoning
from the time it has been intimated to us (or to our justiciar, if
we should be out of the realm), the four barons aforesaid shall refer
that matter to the rest of the five-and-twenty barons, and those

five-and-twenty barons shall, together with the community of the whole

land, distrain and distress us in all possible ways, namely, by seizing

our castles, lands, possessions, and in any other way they can, until redress has been obtained as they deem fit, saving harmless our own

person, and the persons of our queen and children; and when redress has

been obtained, they shall resume their old relations toward us. And let

whoever in the country desires it, swear to obey the orders of the said

five-and-twenty barons for the execution of all the aforesaid matters, and along with them, to molest us to the utmost of his power; and we

publicly and freely grant leave to every one who wishes to swear, and

we shall never forbid any one to swear. All those, moreover, in the land who of themselves and of their own accord are unwilling to swear

to the twenty-five to help them in constraining and molesting us, we shall by our command compel the same to swear to the effect aforesaid.

And if any one of the five-and-twenty barons shall have died or departed from the land, or be incapacitated in any other manner which

would prevent the foresaid provisions being carried out, those of the said twenty-five barons who are left shall choose another in his place according to their own judgment, and he shall be sworn in the same way as the others. Further, in all matters, the execution of which

is intrusted to these twenty-five barons, if perchance these twenty-five are present, that which the majority of those present

ordain or command shall be held as fixed and established, exactly as if
the whole twenty-five had concurred in this; and the said twenty-five
shall swear that they will faithfully observe all that is aforesaid,
and cause it to be observed with all their might. And we shall procure
nothing from any one, directly or indirectly, whereby any part of
these concessions and liberties might be revoked or diminished; and if
any such thing has been procured, let it be void and null, and we shall
never use it personally or by another.

62. And all the ill-will, hatreds, and bitterness that have arisen
between us and our men, clergy and lay, from the date of the quarrel,
we have completely remitted and pardoned every one. Moreover, all
trespasses occasioned by the said quarrel, from Easter in the sixteenth
year of our reign till the restoration of peace, we have fully remitted
to all, both clergy and laymen, and completely forgiven, as far as
pertains to us. And, on this head, we have caused to be made for them
letters testimonial patent of the lord Stephen, archbishop of
Canterbury, of the lord Henry, archbishop of Dublin, of the bishops
aforesaid, and of Master Pandulf as touching this security and
the concessions aforesaid.

63. Wherefore it is our will, and we firmly enjoin, that the English
Church be free, and that the men in our kingdom have and hold all the
aforesaid liberties, rights, and concessions, well and peaceably,
freely and quietly, fully and wholly, for themselves and their heirs,
of us and our heirs, in all respects and in all places for ever, as is

aforesaid. An oath, moreover, has been taken, as well on our part as on
the part of the barons, that all these conditions aforesaid shall be kept in good faith and without evil intent. Given under our hand--the above-named and many others being witnesses--in the meadow which is
called Runnymede, between Windsor and Staines, on the fifteenth day of
June, in the seventeenth year of our reign.

***

The text of THE MAGNA CARTA

The Magna Carta (The Great Charter):

Preamble:

John, by the grace of God, king of England, lord of Ireland, duke of Normandy and Aquitaine, and count of Anjou, to the archbishop, bishops, abbots, earls, barons, justiciaries, foresters, sheriffs, stewards, servants, and to all his bailiffs and liege subjects, greetings.   Know that, having regard to God and for the salvation of our soul, and those of all our ancestors and heirs, and unto the honor
of God and the advancement of his holy Church and for the rectifying
of our realm, we have granted as underwritten by advice of our venerable fathers, Stephen, archbishop of Canterbury, primate of all England and cardinal of the holy Roman Church, Henry, archbishop of

Dublin, William of London, Peter of Winchester, Jocelyn of Bath and Glastonbury, Hugh of Lincoln, Walter of Worcester, William of Coventry, Benedict of Rochester, bishops; of Master Pandulf, subdeacon
and member of the household of our lord the Pope, of brother Aymeric
(master of the Knights of the Temple in England), and of the illustrious men William Marshal, earl of Pembroke, William, earl of Salisbury, William, earl of Warenne, William, earl of Arundel, Alan of Galloway (constable of Scotland), Waren Fitz Gerold, Peter Fitz Herbert, Hubert De Burgh (seneschal of Poitou), Hugh de Neville, Matthew Fitz Herbert, Thomas Basset, Alan Basset, Philip d'Aubigny,
Robert of Roppesley, John Marshal, John Fitz Hugh, and others, our liegemen.

1. In the first place we have granted to God, and by this our present charter confirmed for us and our heirs forever that the English Church
shall be free, and shall have her rights entire, and her liberties inviolate; and we will that it be thus observed; which is apparent from this that the freedom of elections, which is reckoned most important and very essential to the English Church, we, of our pure and unconstrained will, did grant, and did by our charter confirm and did obtain the ratification of the same from our lord, Pope Innocent III, before the quarrel arose between us and our barons: and this we will observe, and our will is that it be observed in good faith by our heirs forever.   We have also granted to all freemen of our kingdom, for us and our heirs forever, all the underwritten liberties, to be had and held by them and their heirs, of us and our heirs forever.

2. If any of our earls or barons, or others holding of us in chief by military service shall have died, and at the time of his death his

heir shall be full of age and owe "relief", he shall have his inheritance by the old relief, to wit, the heir or heirs of an earl, for the whole baroncy of an earl by L100; the heir or heirs of a baron, L100 for a whole barony; the heir or heirs of a knight, 100s, at most, and whoever owes less let him give less, according to the ancient custom of fees.

3. If, however, the heir of any one of the aforesaid has been under age and in wardship, let him have his inheritance without relief and without fine when he comes of age.

4. The guardian of the land of an heir who is thus under age, shall take from the land of the heir nothing but reasonable produce, reasonable customs, and reasonable services, and that without destruction or waste of men or goods; and if we have committed the wardship of the lands of any such minor to the sheriff, or to any other who is responsible to us for its issues, and he has made destruction or waster of what he holds in wardship, we will take of him amends, and the land shall be committed to two lawful and discreet
men of that fee, who shall be responsible for the issues to us or to him to whom we shall assign them; and if we have given or sold the wardship of any such land to anyone and he has therein made destruction or waste, he shall lose that wardship, and it shall be transferred to two lawful and discreet men of that fief, who shall be responsible to us in like manner as aforesaid.

5. The guardian, moreover, so long as he has the wardship of the land,
shall keep up the houses, parks, fishponds, stanks, mills, and other things pertaining to the land, out of the issues of the same land; and he shall restore to the heir, when he has come to full age, all his

land, stocked with ploughs and wainage, according as the season of husbandry shall require, and the issues of the land can reasonable bear.

6. Heirs shall be married without disparagement, yet so that before the marriage takes place the nearest in blood to that heir shall have notice.

7. A widow, after the death of her husband, shall forthwith and without difficulty have her marriage portion and inheritance; nor shall she give anything for her dower, or for her marriage portion, or for the inheritance which her husband and she held on the day of the
death of that husband; and she may remain in the house of her husband
for forty days after his death, within which time her dower shall be assigned to her.

8. No widow shall be compelled to marry, so long as she prefers to live without a husband; provided always that she gives security not to
marry without our consent, if she holds of us, or without the consent of the lord of whom she holds, if she holds of another.

9. Neither we nor our bailiffs will seize any land or rent for any debt, as long as the chattels of the debtor are sufficient to repay the debt; nor shall the sureties of the debtor be distrained so long as the principal debtor is able to satisfy the debt; and if the principal debtor shall fail to pay the debt, having nothing wherewith to pay it, then the sureties shall answer for the debt; and let them have the lands and rents of the debtor, if they desire them, until they are indemnified for the debt which they have paid for him, unless
the principal debtor can show proof that he is discharged thereof as

against the said sureties.

10. If one who has borrowed from the Jews any sum, great or small, die
before that loan be repaid, the debt shall not bear interest while the
heir is under age, of whomsoever he may hold; and if the debt fall
into our hands, we will not take anything except the principal sum
contained in the bond.

11. And if anyone die indebted to the Jews, his wife shall have her
dower and pay nothing of that debt; and if any children of the
deceased are left under age, necessaries shall be provided for them
in
keeping with the holding of the deceased; and out of the residue the
debt shall be paid, reserving, however, service due to feudal lords;
in like manner let it be done touching debts due to others than Jews.

12. No scutage not aid shall be imposed on our kingdom, unless by
common counsel of our kingdom, except for ransoming our person,
for
making our eldest son a knight, and for once marrying our eldest
daughter; and for these there shall not be levied more than a
reasonable aid.   In like manner it shall be done concerning aids
from
the city of London.

13. And the city of London shall have all it ancient liberties and
free customs, as well by land as by water; furthermore, we decree
and grant that all other cities, boroughs, towns, and ports shall
have all their liberties and free customs.

14. And for obtaining the common counsel of the kingdom anent the
assessing of an aid (except in the three cases aforesaid) or of a
scutage, we will cause to be summoned the archbishops, bishops,

abbots, earls, and greater barons, severally by our letters; and we
will moveover cause to be summoned generally, through our sheriffs
and
bailiffs, and others who hold of us in chief, for a fixed date,
namely, after the expiry of at least forty days, and at a fixed place;
and in all letters of such summons we will specify the reason of the
summons.   And when the summons has thus been made, the
business shall
proceed on the day appointed, according to the counsel of such as
are
present, although not all who were summoned have come.

15. We will not for the future grant to anyone license to take an aid
from his own free tenants, except to ransom his person, to make his
eldest son a knight, and once to marry his eldest daughter; and on
each of these occasions there shall be levied only a reasonable aid.

16. No one shall be distrained for performance of greater service for
a knight's fee, or for any other free tenement, than is due therefrom.

17. Common pleas shall not follow our court, but shall be held in
some
fixed place.

18. Inquests of novel disseisin, of mort d'ancestor, and of darrein
presentment shall not be held elsewhere than in their own county
courts, and that in manner following; We, or, if we should be out of
the realm, our chief justiciar, will send two justiciaries through
every county four times a year, who shall alone with four knights of
the county chosen by the county, hold the said assizes in the county
court, on the day and in the place of meeting of that court.

19. And if any of the said assizes cannot be taken on the day of the
county court, let there remain of the knights and freeholders, who

were present at the county court on that day, as many as may be required for the efficient making of judgments, according as the business be more or less.

20. A freeman shall not be amerced for a slight offense, except in accordance with the degree of the offense; and for a grave offense he
shall be amerced in accordance with the gravity of the offense, yet saving always his "contentment"; and a merchant in the same way, saving his "merchandise"; and a villein shall be amerced in the same
way, saving his "wainage" if they have fallen into our mercy: and none
of the aforesaid amercements shall be imposed except by the oath of
honest men of the neighborhood.

21. Earls and barons shall not be amerced except through their peers,
and only in accordance with the degree of the offense.

22. A clerk shall not be amerced in respect of his lay holding except after the manner of the others aforesaid; further, he shall not be amerced in accordance with the extent of his ecclesiastical benefice.

23. No village or individual shall be compelled to make bridges at river banks, except those who from of old were legally bound to do so.

24. No sheriff, constable, coroners, or others of our bailiffs, shall hold pleas of our Crown.

25. All counties, hundred, wapentakes, and trithings (except our demesne manors) shall remain at the old rents, and without any

additional payment.

26. If anyone holding of us a lay fief shall die, and our sheriff or bailiff shall exhibit our letters patent of summons for a debt which the deceased owed us, it shall be lawful for our sheriff or bailiff to attach and enroll the chattels of the deceased, found upon the lay fief, to the value of that debt, at the sight of law worthy men, provided always that nothing whatever be thence removed until the debt
which is evident shall be fully paid to us; and the residue shall be left to the executors to fulfill the will of the deceased; and if
there be nothing due from him to us, all the chattels shall go to the deceased, saving to his wife and children their reasonable shares.

27. If any freeman shall die intestate, his chattels shall be distributed by the hands of his nearest kinsfolk and friends, under supervision of the Church, saving to every one the debts which the deceased owed to him.

28. No constable or other bailiff of ours shall take corn or other provisions from anyone without immediately tendering money therefor,
unless he can have postponement thereof by permission of the seller.

29. No constable shall compel any knight to give money in lieu of castle-guard, when he is willing to perform it in his own person, or (if he himself cannot do it from any reasonable cause) then by another
responsible man.   Further, if we have led or sent him upon military service, he shall be relieved from guard in proportion to the time during which he has been on service because of us.

30. No sheriff or bailiff of ours, or other person, shall take the

horses or carts of any freeman for transport duty, against the will of the said freeman.

31. Neither we nor our bailiffs shall take, for our castles or for any other work of ours, wood which is not ours, against the will of the owner of that wood.

32. We will not retain beyond one year and one day, the lands those who have been convicted of felony, and the lands shall thereafter be handed over to the lords of the fiefs.

33. All kydells for the future shall be removed altogether from Thames
and Medway, and throughout all England, except upon the seashore.

34. The writ which is called praecipe shall not for the future be issued to anyone, regarding any tenement whereby a freeman may lose
his court.

35. Let there be one measure of wine throughout our whole realm; and
one measure of ale; and one measure of corn, to wit, "the London quarter"; and one width of cloth (whether dyed, or russet, or "halberget"), to wit, two ells within the selvedges; of weights also let it be as of measures.

36. Nothing in future shall be given or taken for a writ of inquisition of life or limbs, but freely it shall be granted, and never denied.

37. If anyone holds of us by fee-farm, either by socage or by burage, or of any other land by knight's service, we will not (by reason of

that fee-farm, socage, or burgage), have the wardship of the heir, or of such land of his as if of the fief of that other; nor shall we have wardship of that fee-farm, socage, or burgage, unless such fee-farm owes knight's service.   We will not by reason of any small serjeancy
which anyone may hold of us by the service of rendering to us knives,
arrows, or the like, have wardship of his heir or of the land which he holds of another lord by knight's service.

38. No bailiff for the future shall, upon his own unsupported complaint, put anyone to his "law", without credible witnesses brought
for this purposes.

39. No freemen shall be taken or imprisoned or disseised or exiled or
in any way destroyed, nor will we go upon him nor send upon him, except by the lawful judgment of his peers or by the law of the land.

40. To no one will we sell, to no one will we refuse or delay, right or justice.

41. All merchants shall have safe and secure exit from England, and entry to England, with the right to tarry there and to move about as well by land as by water, for buying and selling by the ancient and right customs, quit from all evil tolls, except (in time of war) such merchants as are of the land at war with us. And if such are found in our land at the beginning of the war, they shall be detained, without injury to their bodies or goods, until information be received by us, or by our chief justiciar, how the merchants of our land found in the land at war with us are treated; and if our men are safe there, the others shall be safe in our land.

42. It shall be lawful in future for anyone (excepting always those imprisoned or outlawed in accordance with the law of the kingdom, and
natives of any country at war with us, and merchants, who shall be treated as if above provided) to leave our kingdom and to return, safe
and secure by land and water, except for a short period in time of war, on grounds of public policy- reserving always the allegiance due
to us.

43. If anyone holding of some escheat (such as the honor of Wallingford, Nottingham, Boulogne, Lancaster, or of other escheats which are in our hands and are baronies) shall die, his heir shall give no other relief, and perform no other service to us than he would
have done to the baron if that barony had been in the baron's hand; and we shall hold it in the same manner in which the baron held it.

44. Men who dwell without the forest need not henceforth come before
our justiciaries of the forest upon a general summons, unless they are
in plea, or sureties of one or more, who are attached for the forest.

45. We will appoint as justices, constables, sheriffs, or bailiffs only such as know the law of the realm and mean to observe it well.

46. All barons who have founded abbeys, concerning which they hold
charters from the kings of England, or of which they have long continued possession, shall have the wardship of them, when vacant, as
they ought to have.

47. All forests that have been made such in our time shall forthwith be disafforsted; and a similar course shall be followed with regard to river banks that have been placed "in defense" by us in our time.

48.   All evil customs connected with forests and warrens, foresters and warreners, sheriffs and their officers, river banks and their wardens, shall immediately by inquired into in each county by twelve sworn knights of the same county chosen by the honest men of the same
county, and shall, within forty days of the said inquest, be utterly abolished, so as never to be restored, provided always that we previously have intimation thereof, or our justiciar, if we should not be in England.

49. We will immediately restore all hostages and charters delivered to
us by Englishmen, as sureties of the peace of faithful service.

50. We will entirely remove from their bailiwicks, the relations of Gerard of Athee (so that in future they shall have no bailiwick in England); namely, Engelard of Cigogne, Peter, Guy, and Andrew of Chanceaux, Guy of Cigogne, Geoffrey of Martigny with his brothers, Philip Mark with his brothers and his nephew Geoffrey, and the whole
brood of the same.

51. As soon as peace is restored, we will banish from the kingdom all
foreign born knights, crossbowmen, serjeants, and mercenary soldiers
who have come with horses and arms to the kingdom's hurt.

52. If anyone has been dispossessed or removed by us, without the

legal judgment of his peers, from his lands, castles, franchises, or from his right, we will immediately restore them to him; and if a dispute arise over this, then let it be decided by the five and twenty barons of whom mention is made below in the clause for securing the

peace.   Moreover, for all those possessions, from which anyone has,

without the lawful judgment of his peers, been disseised or removed, by our father, King Henry, or by our brother, King Richard, and which

we retain in our hand (or which as possessed by others, to whom we are

bound to warrant them) we shall have respite until the usual term of crusaders; excepting those things about which a plea has been raised,

or an inquest made by our order, before our taking of the cross; but as soon as we return from the expedition, we will immediately grant full justice therein.

53. We shall have, moreover, the same respite and in the same manner

in rendering justice concerning the disafforestation or retention of those forests which Henry our father and Richard our brother afforested, and concerning the wardship of lands which are of the fief

of another (namely, such wardships as we have hitherto had by reason

of a fief which anyone held of us by knight's service), and concerning

abbeys founded on other fiefs than our own, in which the lord of the fee claims to have right; and when we have returned, or if we desist from our expedition, we will immediately grant full justice to all who complain of such things.

54. No one shall be arrested or imprisoned upon the appeal of a woman,
for the death of any other than her husband.

55. All fines made with us unjustly and against the law of the land, and all amercements, imposed unjustly and against the law of the land,
shall be entirely remitted, or else it shall be done concerning them according to the decision of the five and twenty barons whom mention
is made below in the clause for securing the pease, or according to the judgment of the majority of the same, along with the aforesaid Stephen, archbishop of Canterbury, if he can be present, and such others as he may wish to bring with him for this purpose, and if he cannot be present the business shall nevertheless proceed without him,
provided always that if any one or more of the aforesaid five and twenty barons are in a similar suit, they shall be removed as far as concerns this particular judgment, others being substituted in their places after having been selected by the rest of the same five and twenty for this purpose only, and after having been sworn.

56. If we have disseised or removed Welshmen from lands or liberties,
or other things, without the legal judgment of their peers in England or in Wales, they shall be immediately restored to them; and if a dispute arise over this, then let it be decided in the marches by the judgment of their peers; for the tenements in England according to the
law of England, for tenements in Wales according to the law of Wales,
and for tenements in the marches according to the law of the marches.
Welshmen shall do the same to us and ours.

57. Further, for all those possessions from which any Welshman
has,
without the lawful judgment of his peers, been disseised or removed
by
King Henry our father, or King Richard our brother, and which we
retain in our hand (or which are possessed by others, and which we
ought to warrant), we will have respite until the usual term of
crusaders; excepting those things about which a plea has been
raised
or an inquest made by our order before we took the cross; but as
soon
as we return (or if perchance we desist from our expedition), we will
immediately grant full justice in accordance with the laws of the
Welsh and in relation to the foresaid regions.

58. We will immediately give up the son of Llywelyn and all the
hostages of Wales, and the charters delivered to us as security for
the peace.

59. We will do towards Alexander, king of Scots, concerning the
return
of his sisters and his hostages, and concerning his franchises, and
his right, in the same manner as we shall do towards our other
barons
of England, unless it ought to be otherwise according to the charters
which we hold from William his father, formerly king of Scots; and
this shall be according to the judgment of his peers in our court.

60. Moreover, all these aforesaid customs and liberties, the
observances of which we have granted in our kingdom as far as
pertains
to us towards our men, shall be observed b all of our kingdom, as
well

clergy as laymen, as far as pertains to them towards their men.

61. Since, moveover, for God and the amendment of our kingdom and for
the better allaying of the quarrel that has arisen between us and our barons, we have granted all these concessions, desirous that they should enjoy them in complete and firm endurance forever, we give and
grant to them the underwritten security, namely, that the barons choose five and twenty barons of the kingdom, whomsoever they will,
who shall be bound with all their might, to observe and hold, and cause to be observed, the peace and liberties we have granted and confirmed to them by this our present Charter, so that if we, or our justiciar, or our bailiffs or any one of our officers, shall in anything be at fault towards anyone, or shall have broken any one of
the articles of this peace or of this security, and the offense be notified to four barons of the foresaid five and twenty, the said four barons shall repair to us (or our justiciar, if we are out of the realm) and, laying the transgression before us, petition to have that transgression redressed without delay.   And if we shall not have corrected the transgression (or, in the event of our being out of the realm, if our justiciar shall not have corrected it) within forty days, reckoning from the time it has been intimated to us (or to our justiciar, if we should be out of the realm), the four barons aforesaid shall refer that matter to the rest of the five and twenty barons, and those five and twenty barons shall, together with the community of the whole realm, distrain and distress us in all possible
ways, namely, by seizing our castles, lands, possessions, and in any
other way they can, until redress has been obtained as they deem fit, saving harmless our own person, and the persons of our queen and

children; and when redress has been obtained, they shall resume their

old relations towards us.   And let whoever in the country desires it, swear to obey the orders of the said five and twenty barons for the execution of all the aforesaid matters, and along with them, to molest

us to the utmost of his power; and we publicly and freely grant leave to everyone who wishes to swear, and we shall never forbid anyone to

swear.

All those, moveover, in the land who of themselves and of their own accord are unwilling to swear to the twenty five to help them in constraining and molesting us, we shall by our command compel the same

to swear to the effect foresaid.   And if any one of the five and twenty barons shall have died or departed from the land, or be incapacitated in any other manner which would prevent the foresaid provisions being carried out, those of the said twenty five barons who

are left shall choose another in his place according to their own judgment, and he shall be sworn in the same way as the others. Further, in all matters, the execution of which is entrusted,to these twenty five barons, if perchance these twenty five are present and disagree about anything, or if some of them, after being summoned, are

unwilling or unable to be present, that which the majority of those present ordain or command shall be held as fixed and established, exactly as if the whole twenty five had concurred in this; and the said twenty five shall swear that they will faithfully observe all that is aforesaid, and cause it to be observed with all their might. And we shall procure nothing from anyone, directly or indirectly, whereby any part of these concessions and liberties might be revoked or diminished; and if any such things has been procured, let it be void and null, and we shall never use it personally or by another.

62. And all the will, hatreds, and bitterness that have arisen between us and our men, clergy and lay, from the date of the quarrel, we have
completely remitted and pardoned to everyone.   Moreover, all trespasses occasioned by the said quarrel, from Easter in the sixteenth year of our reign till the restoration of peace, we have fully remitted to all, both clergy and laymen, and completely forgiven, as far as pertains to us.   And on this head, we have caused
to be made for them letters testimonial patent of the lord Stephen, archbishop of Canterbury, of the lord Henry, archbishop of Dublin, of the bishops aforesaid, and of Master Pandulf as touching this security
and the concessions aforesaid.

63. Wherefore we will and firmly order that the English Church be free, and that the men in our kingdom have and hold all the aforesaid
liberties, rights, and concessions, well and peaceably, freely and quietly, fully and wholly, for themselves and their heirs, of us and our heirs, in all respects and in all places forever, as is
aforesaid.   An oath, moreover, has been taken, as well on our part as
on the part of the barons, that all these conditions aforesaid shall be kept in good faith and without evil intent.   Given under our hand - the above named and many others being witnesses - in the meadow which
is called Runnymede, between Windsor and Staines, on the fifteenth day
of June, in the seventeenth year of our reign.

***

Made in the USA
Coppell, TX
05 October 2020

39325112R00031